T0063366

A HANDFUL *of* LOVE

Haiku's for Every Season

SAMUEL C. WILLIAMS

PARTRIDGE

A Penguin Random House Company

To order additional copies of this book, contact
Toll Free 800 101 2657 (Singapore)
Toll Free 1 800 81 7340 (Malaysia)
orders.singapore@partridgepublishing.com

www.partridgepublishing.com/singapore

About the Author

Samuel C. Williams, III is a long time writer. Reportedly he wrote his first book, a short children's story, at the age of seven years old when he was only in second grade. Nearly all of his teachers from elementary school through college saw the love and unbridled passion he possessed for reading and writing and often prognosticated that his future would be one that was writing centered. As fate would have it, the prognosticators were right. Upon graduating Wadley High School (Wadley, GA) in 1973, he entered Paine College and remained there until his 1977 graduation with a BA degree in English. Upon earning his degree from Paine College, Williams entered the U.S. Army as a military journalist. Again fate struck positively in Williams' life and career as for the next several years he served in "special duty" assignments. During these years he served as a journalist with the 44th Military Historical Detachment, was allowed to return to school to complete advanced public affairs and photojournalism training, served as the lead staff writer for the Ft. McPherson Sentinel and as a contributing journalist to the U.S. Army Forces Command weekly paper. Williams also covered professional sports and all cultural events for the papers and also served as the lead staff writer for the Berlin Brigade. The busy writer also simultaneously served as a senior U.S. Army public affairs official in the U.S. Consulate there in Berlin. Williams refused an offer by the Army to attend its then highest journalism and public affairs training available, a fully funded graduate program of study at the prestigious Syracuse University School of Journalism and Public Affairs (Syracuse, NY) and departed Berlin in 1982 to attend the Army's Officer Candidate School (OCS) at Ft. Benning, GA. Williams graduated OCS and was commissioned a second lieutenant in the U.S. Army in 1982. A student of continual learning, Williams persisted in his pursuit of learning and knowledge. He has since attended and completed several schools and has also earned two advanced degrees. Williams is the husband of Sharleeen E. B. Williams, the father of two wonderful offsprings, Samuel IV and Shundalynn, and two irresistible granddaughters, Jordyn and LeAndre Williams. Williams is also the author of My Pen, His Thoughts, See My Purpose:20 Plays, 30 Days to a Better You—Guaranteed, and several other works. Known throughout for his great inspirational and motivational speaking, this dynamic penman can be contacted via email at manifestnow1@yahoo.com or by writing to PSC 473 Box 3014, FPO, AP 96349.

Foreword

There is nothing more fun in the entire profession of teaching than to see the eyes of a once perplexed student light up and his mouth announce to the world, "Oh! Oh! I see now. Now I understand what you're saying." It's moments such as this for which all teachers live. No teacher teaches simply to administer examines and to do paper work. All of that just happens to come along with the job. And because we love the job, we'll gladly take on the other tasks as well.

Teaching is a passion of mine. In all that I do and in all that I am, I am first and foremost a teacher and I seek to always do what I am. As a result, teaching has clearly taught me that students are more likely to re-produce what they are taught in combination with what they see and hear—thus this book. It is easy to tell students to write a 5-7-5 Haiku poem and maybe to write three, four or five "really good ones" for a grade. But is it as easy to teach students that they are capable of writing really meaningful Haiku poems on nearly any subject given them? And why would they believe you even if you did say so?

Well, the basis for all such arguments are totally eradicated in all of my classes. My students are instructed in the arts of writing essays, but only after I pass around model essays that I've personally written for them to see. My students read and to hear analyze dramatic works throughout the year, but only after I've introduced them to drama and its myriad concepts through one or several of the many plays I have written for the classroom just for such a purpose. Students are not told to pull out laptops and research the internet for the history and types of haiku poems until I first share several haikus with them that I have written.

This book represents one such effort on my part again. In this book I have taken any number of mundane topics and have turned them into independent haiku works. Though short, within each poem, the reader will, with minimum effort and thought, readily unveil numerous life's lessons and teachings. I am hopeful you will take the time to read each of them and that your heart as well as your mind will readily grasp the truths contained in each of them.

Introduction

There's nothing like being short, sweet and to the point. My grandfather, an old southern minister and pastor, preached many awesome sermons, however, most of them usually lasted only around fifteen to twenty minutes. One day I went to him and asked, "Granddaddy, why don't you say more when you preach? Why are you always so swift and short when you preach?"

My grandfather quickly retorted," There's no need to be long when being short and swift will work just as well. Long is only needed when short won't do. To give a good, profound and powerful message, son," he taught me, "there are only two principles one need observe. The first being the rule of the "ups": get up, speak up and shut up. The other principle is to ensure your message complies with the Rules of the P's."

The Rule of the P's? What is that, Grandpa? I inquired.

"In order for your message to have a lasting impact on people, it must be personal, portable and practical. There must be something in it with which each person can personally identify. Then you have to make sure that that with which they identify becomes portable within them. They must be able to walk away from the comfort and security of the speaker and yet conceal and carry the essence of what they just heard with them no matter where they are from or where they are going. And finally, that which becomes portable must also become instantly practical. That is they must be able to make practical application of the principles that they have ported and made a personal part of their lives.

His fifteen to twenty minutes of teaching were now up and so were my teachable moments for the day. My grandfather walked away, but his very practical, personal and portable message had reaped great benefits with me already. And today, I present this very personal, practical and portable method of teaching students valuable life's lessons via the use of haiku poetry. I sincerely hope you learn from them, enjoy them and pass them on to all whom you meet.

Why Haiku?

Haiku poems are believed to have come into existence between the 19th and the 20th centuries. The Japanese poet and writer Masaoki Shiki is credited with its creation. From their outset, Haiku poems dealt primarily with nature. Over the years they slowly evolved into the addressing of any number of topics, ideas and themes. Today students around the globe write Haiku poems on any number of topics ranging from the most serious to the most light hearted.

Haiku poems are unique in any number of ways. Their three lines seventeen syllable (5-7-5) format is one such example. Nonetheless, it is the beauty and power of these briefly stated compositions which awe Haiku readers again and again.

This is also what I hope to accomplish in this book of Haiku poems. It is my objective to clearly portray to the readers of this book that great and powerful ideas needn't require long and cumbersome writings in order to be succinctly, clearly and impactfully delivered. I pray that each reader of this book will ultimately arrive at the same conviction when s/he is done reading it.

(The poems in his collection are in no specified order.
They appear in random order on each page.)

Puppy Love

Infatuations
They are never what they seem
Enjoy but move on

Growth

Growing into you
Necessary for all things
Do not fear its lead

Choices

We must all make them
No one can escape choosing
Try to. See, you chose

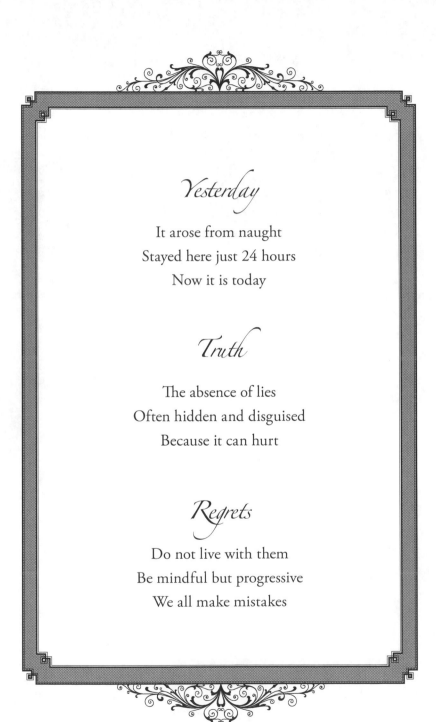

Yesterday

It arose from naught
Stayed here just 24 hours
Now it is today

Truth

The absence of lies
Often hidden and disguised
Because it can hurt

Regrets

Do not live with them
Be mindful but progressive
We all make mistakes

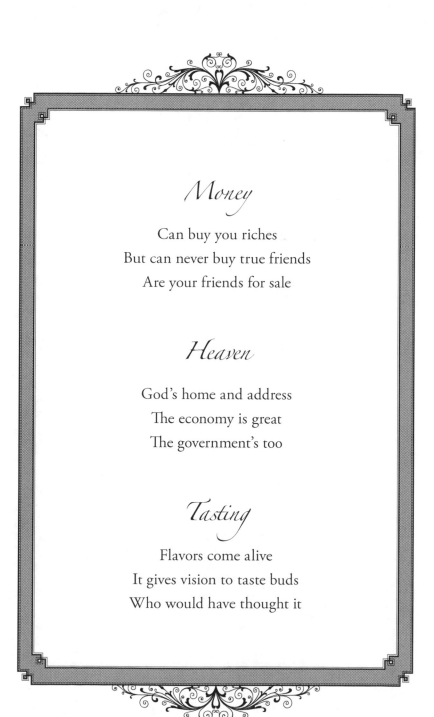

Money

Can buy you riches
But can never buy true friends
Are your friends for sale

Heaven

God's home and address
The economy is great
The government's too

Tasting

Flavors come alive
It gives vision to taste buds
Who would have thought it

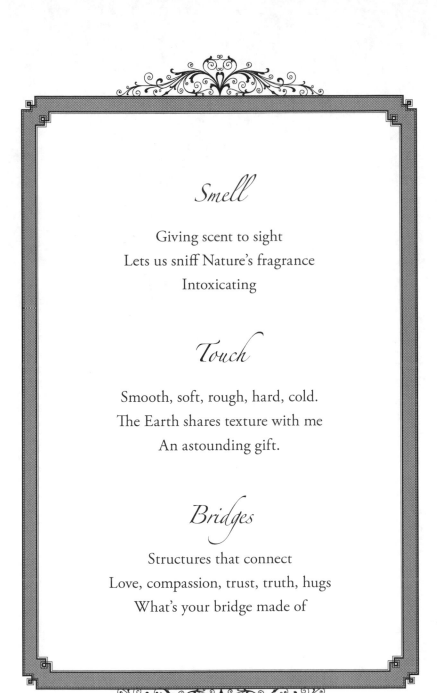

Smell

Giving scent to sight
Lets us sniff Nature's fragrance
Intoxicating

Touch

Smooth, soft, rough, hard, cold.
The Earth shares texture with me
An astounding gift.

Bridges

Structures that connect
Love, compassion, trust, truth, hugs
What's your bridge made of

Smiles

They say I'm ok
And do battle against frowns
They are contagious

Sunrise

The eye of heaven
Finds its place high over head
Then lights all our paths

Sunset

Today is over
The memories are all made
The sun goes to sleep

Moon

Controller of tides
Little brother to the sun
We've visited you

Stars

Splatterings of light
Compasses to all mankind
Some fall and some glow

Trees

Years of pride and strength
With ages like those of rocks
If only they spoke

Flowers

Employers to bees
Beautifiers of the Earth
Fragrance inventor

Birthdays

Old people hate them
Young people love to see them
They just keep coming

Honor

Give it when/where due
Some day you will come due too
Then you'll be honored

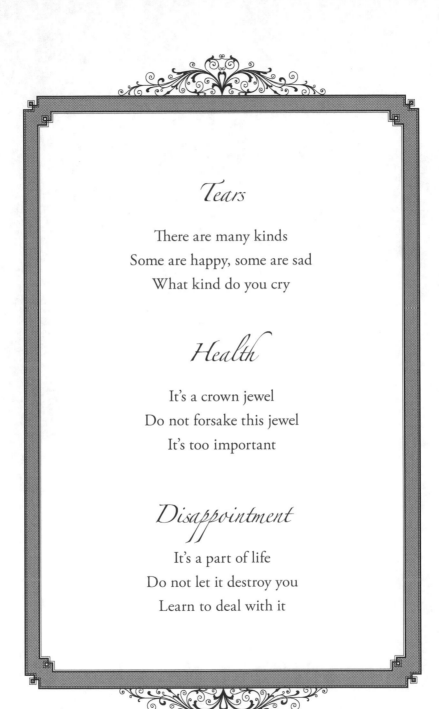

Tears

There are many kinds
Some are happy, some are sad
What kind do you cry

Health

It's a crown jewel
Do not forsake this jewel
It's too important

Disappointment

It's a part of life
Do not let it destroy you
Learn to deal with it

Hurt

It seeks to revenge
Hurting people hurt people
Then ask for sorrow

People

We are all the same
Different skins cover us
We are one essence

Things

Important to us
Their values are deceptive
We will leave them here

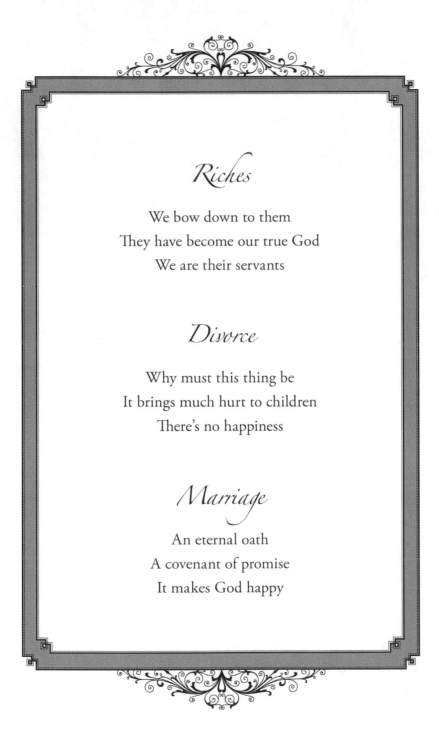

Riches

We bow down to them
They have become our true God
We are their servants

Divorce

Why must this thing be
It brings much hurt to children
There's no happiness

Marriage

An eternal oath
A covenant of promise
It makes God happy

Parenting

Adults' toughest job
Cannot be done by the weak
WANTED: MORE PARENTS

Self

You're the only you
Do not commit suicide
Being someone else

Perfection

No peer or equal
Cannot be improved upon
Is that you by chance

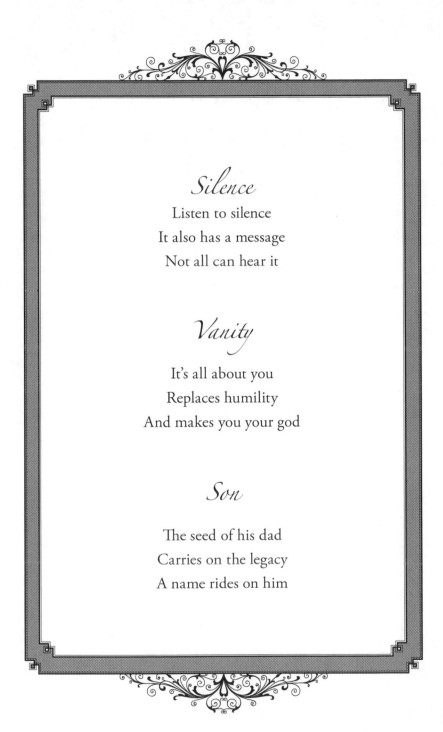

Silence

Listen to silence
It also has a message
Not all can hear it

Vanity

It's all about you
Replaces humility
And makes you your god

Son

The seed of his dad
Carries on the legacy
A name rides on him

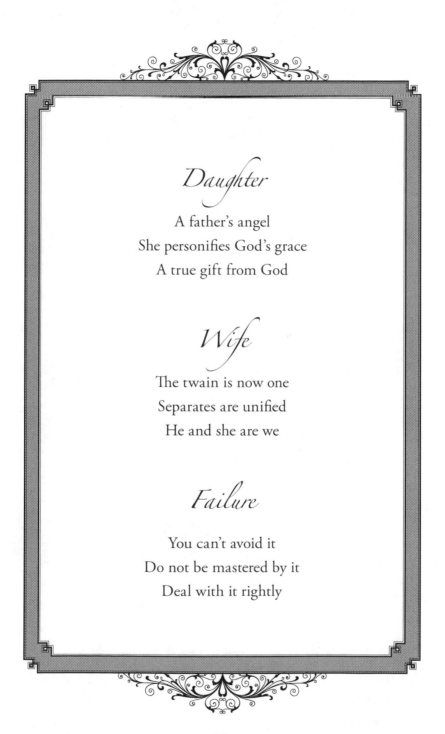

Daughter

A father's angel
She personifies God's grace
A true gift from God

Wife

The twain is now one
Separates are unified
He and she are we

Failure

You can't avoid it
Do not be mastered by it
Deal with it rightly

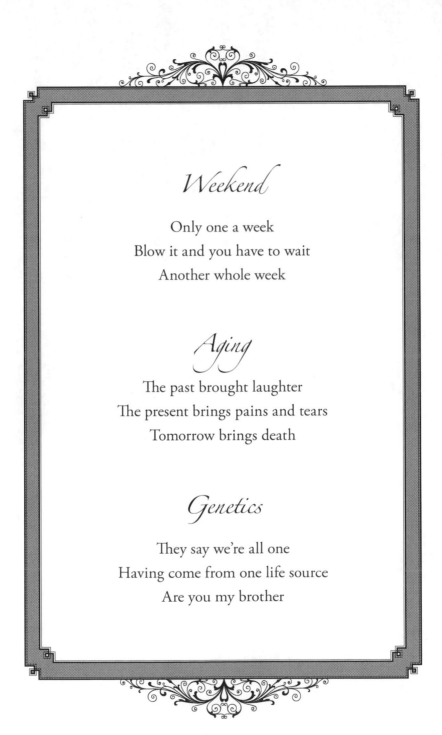

Weekend

Only one a week
Blow it and you have to wait
Another whole week

Aging

The past brought laughter
The present brings pains and tears
Tomorrow brings death

Genetics

They say we're all one
Having come from one life source
Are you my brother

Incarceration

Human behind bars
Caged up in a tiny square
Revenge or justice

Murder

Why kill another
All life is very precious
Give all life respect

Aloneness

You are not lonely
You are just separated
Spending time with you

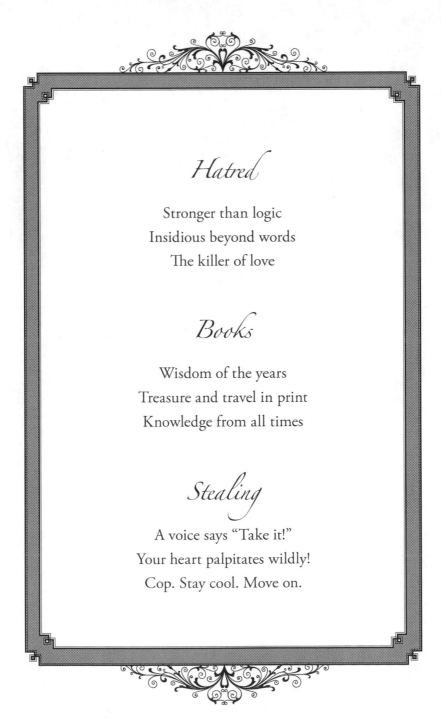

Hatred

Stronger than logic
Insidious beyond words
The killer of love

Books

Wisdom of the years
Treasure and travel in print
Knowledge from all times

Stealing

A voice says "Take it!"
Your heart palpitates wildly!
Cop. Stay cool. Move on.

Death

Some say it's good-bye
No! It's only moving on
It is twin to life

Teachers

Mind cultivators
They shape our future leaders
We should all thank them

Earthquakes

Swaying, trembling, fear
The earth moves under my feet
Bam! Boom! Crash! Oh God!

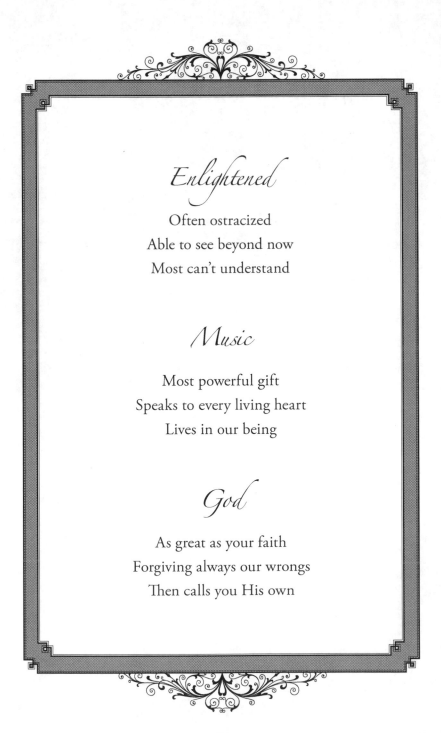

Enlightened

Often ostracized
Able to see beyond now
Most can't understand

Music

Most powerful gift
Speaks to every living heart
Lives in our being

God

As great as your faith
Forgiving always our wrongs
Then calls you His own

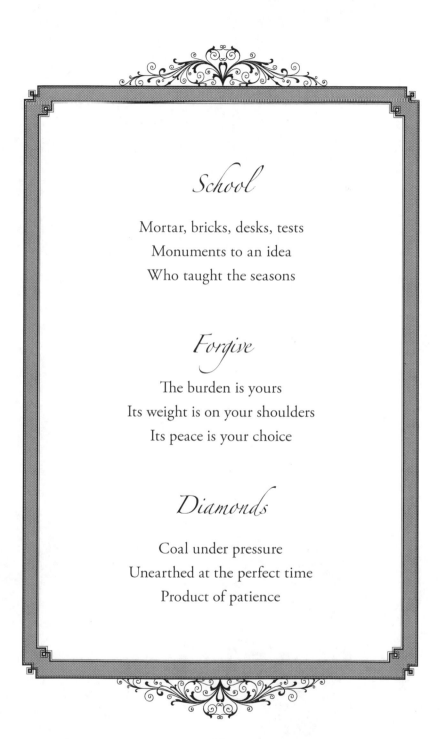

School

Mortar, bricks, desks, tests
Monuments to an idea
Who taught the seasons

Forgive

The burden is yours
Its weight is on your shoulders
Its peace is your choice

Diamonds

Coal under pressure
Unearthed at the perfect time
Product of patience

Gold

Nothing matters more
Men lie, steal and kill for it
Then die and leave it

Laughter

God's own medicine
Brings life to the depressed soul
Makes the spirit smile

Reality

Camouflaged by fakes
Beautiful and plain to see
Many are blinded

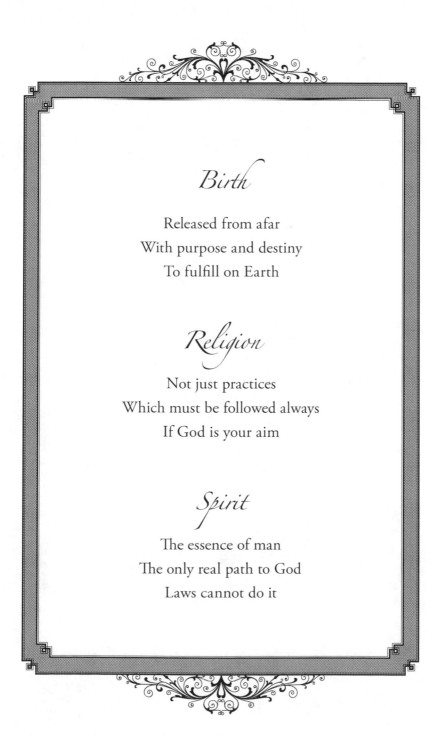

Birth

Released from afar
With purpose and destiny
To fulfill on Earth

Religion

Not just practices
Which must be followed always
If God is your aim

Spirit

The essence of man
The only real path to God
Laws cannot do it

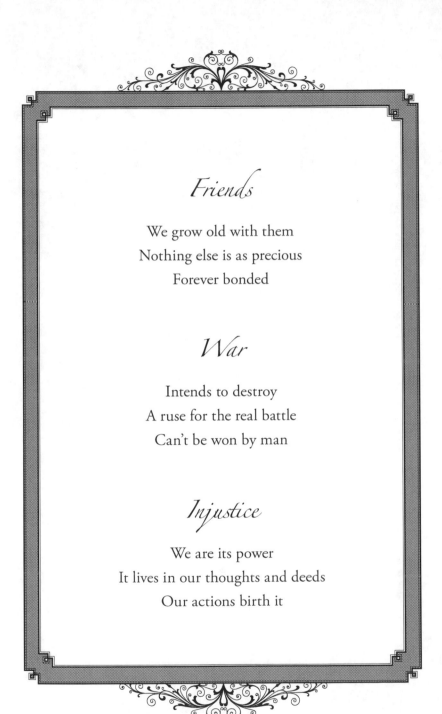

Friends

We grow old with them
Nothing else is as precious
Forever bonded

War

Intends to destroy
A ruse for the real battle
Can't be won by man

Injustice

We are its power
It lives in our thoughts and deeds
Our actions birth it

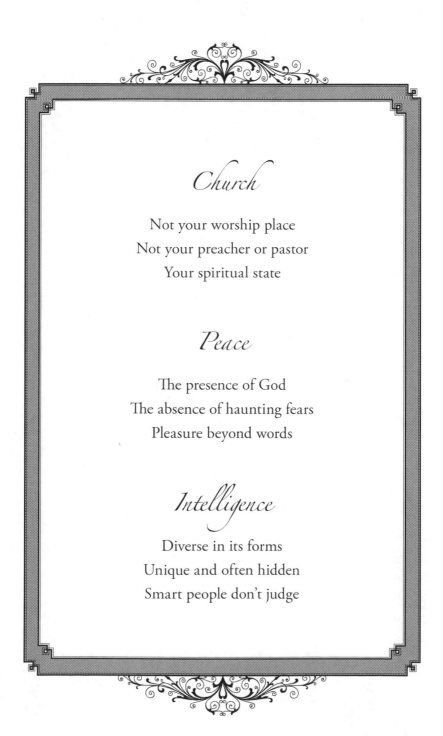

Church

Not your worship place
Not your preacher or pastor
Your spiritual state

Peace

The presence of God
The absence of haunting fears
Pleasure beyond words

Intelligence

Diverse in its forms
Unique and often hidden
Smart people don't judge

Pride

Self-exalting thoughts
Robs people of compassion
Serves only oneself

Wisdom

Forms are light and dark
Don't let the dark deceive you
Light comes from above

Angels

Celestial friends
They protect and guard your way
If you will let them

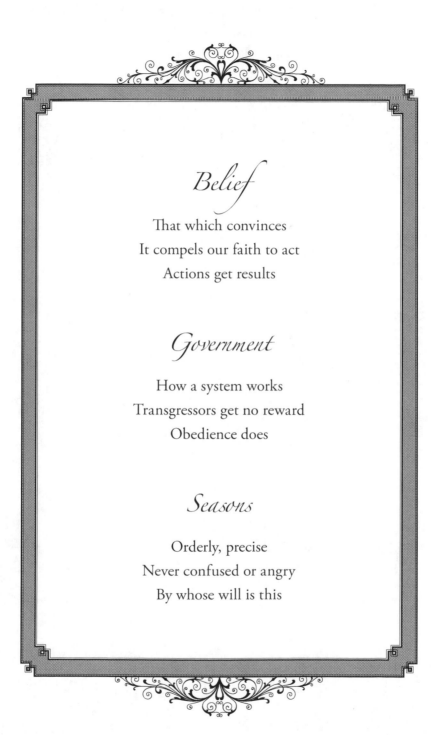

Belief

That which convinces
It compels our faith to act
Actions get results

Government

How a system works
Transgressors get no reward
Obedience does

Seasons

Orderly, precise
Never confused or angry
By whose will is this

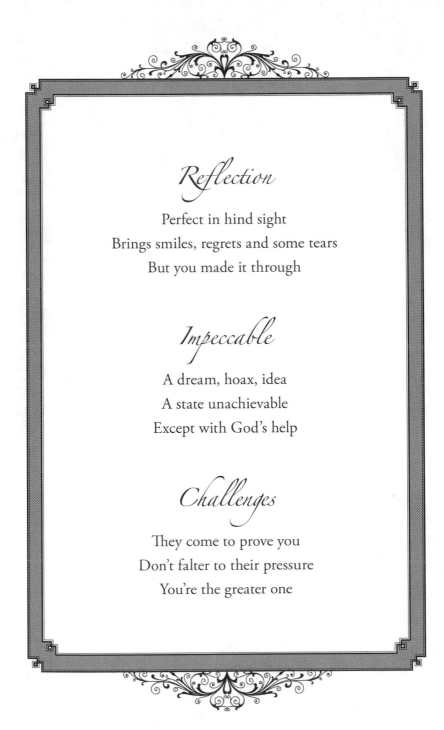

Reflection

Perfect in hind sight
Brings smiles, regrets and some tears
But you made it through

Impeccable

A dream, hoax, idea
A state unachievable
Except with God's help

Challenges

They come to prove you
Don't falter to their pressure
You're the greater one

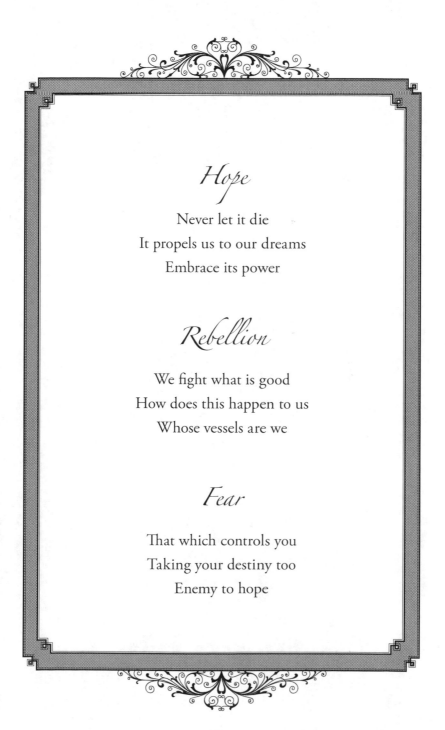

Hope

Never let it die
It propels us to our dreams
Embrace its power

Rebellion

We fight what is good
How does this happen to us
Whose vessels are we

Fear

That which controls you
Taking your destiny too
Enemy to hope

Children

Seeds of our loins
Hope of generations past
Tomorrow's promise

Law

Indispensible
Divinely given by God
To serve only good

Elements

Fire, wind, water
Masterpieces of nature
Who conceived such things

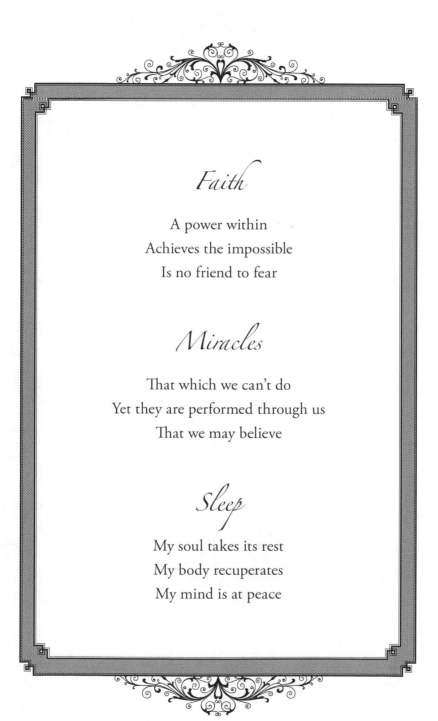

Faith

A power within
Achieves the impossible
Is no friend to fear

Miracles

That which we can't do
Yet they are performed through us
That we may believe

Sleep

My soul takes its rest
My body recuperates
My mind is at peace

Colors

Majestic art work
Revealed to the eyes of man
God at His easel

Spring

The season of birth
The earth's seeds bring forth their fruits
The breath of life breath'd

Summer

Apex of earth's seeds
Culmination of earth's might
Now the seeds declines

Fall

Earth's seeds must now rest
They share the rainbow with us
Then they fall asleep

Winter

Death comes to the earth
Spring awaits its turn again
A new cycle starts

Beauty

That which touches all
It is neither light nor dark
It is . . . what it is

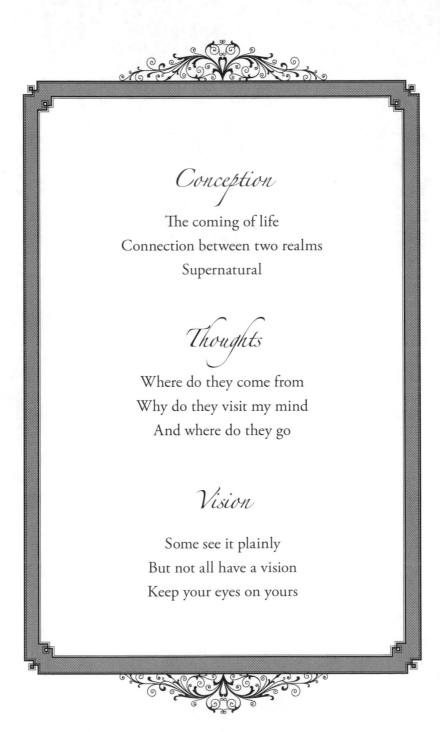

Conception

The coming of life
Connection between two realms
Supernatural

Thoughts

Where do they come from
Why do they visit my mind
And where do they go

Vision

Some see it plainly
But not all have a vision
Keep your eyes on yours

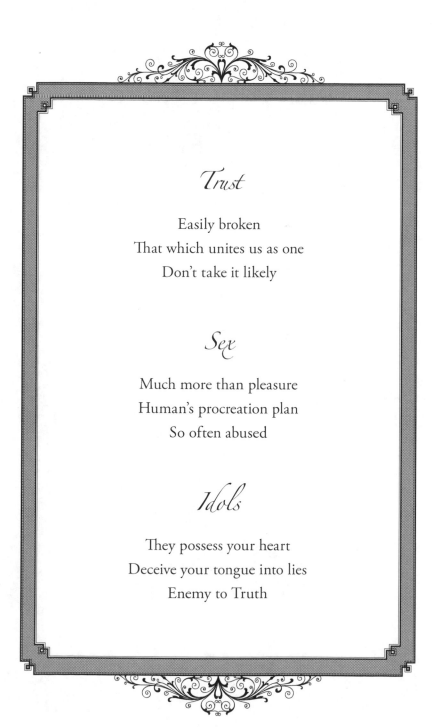

Trust

Easily broken
That which unites us as one
Don't take it likely

Sex

Much more than pleasure
Human's procreation plan
So often abused

Idols

They possess your heart
Deceive your tongue into lies
Enemy to Truth

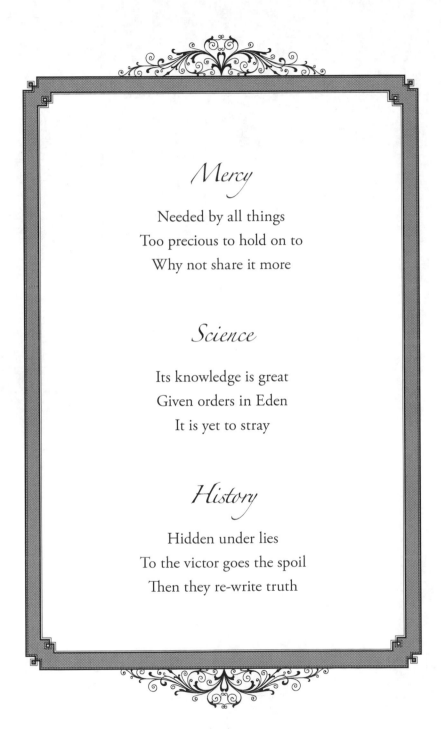

Mercy

Needed by all things
Too precious to hold on to
Why not share it more

Science

Its knowledge is great
Given orders in Eden
It is yet to stray

History

Hidden under lies
To the victor goes the spoil
Then they re-write truth

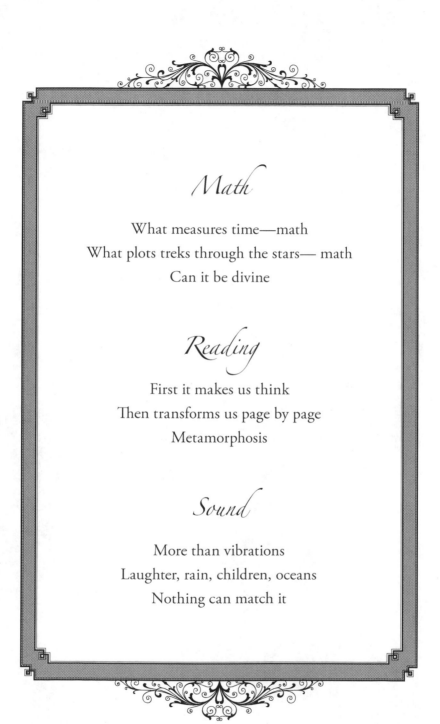

Math

What measures time—math
What plots treks through the stars— math
Can it be divine

Reading

First it makes us think
Then transforms us page by page
Metamorphosis

Sound

More than vibrations
Laughter, rain, children, oceans
Nothing can match it

Butterflies

From beast to beauty
Winged perfection on God's air
Half angel, half man

New Year

Twelve months and one goal
Resolution as my map
Oops! I slipped again

New Shoes

Shiny and sturdy
Make my new suit look better
Too perfect for words

Valentine Day

Flowers everywhere
Chocolate flows like rivers
Card racks are empty

Mothers' Day

Honor her with love
Everyday should be for her
But this one's special

The Ocean

Beauty and power
Cannot be mastered by man
How did it get here

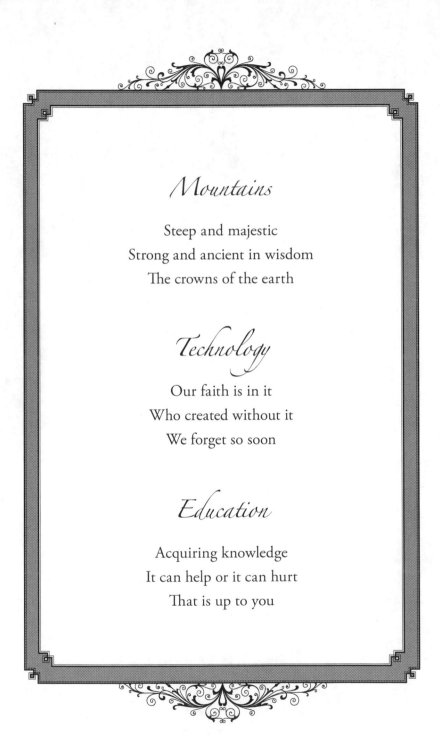

Mountains

Steep and majestic
Strong and ancient in wisdom
The crowns of the earth

Technology

Our faith is in it
Who created without it
We forget so soon

Education

Acquiring knowledge
It can help or it can hurt
That is up to you

Family Reunions

Generations come
Youths are the hope of the old
Elders beam with pride

Funerals

Here is where we part
Grace allowed our paths to cross
None can replace you

College

Freshmen once again
A place of independence
You're growing up now

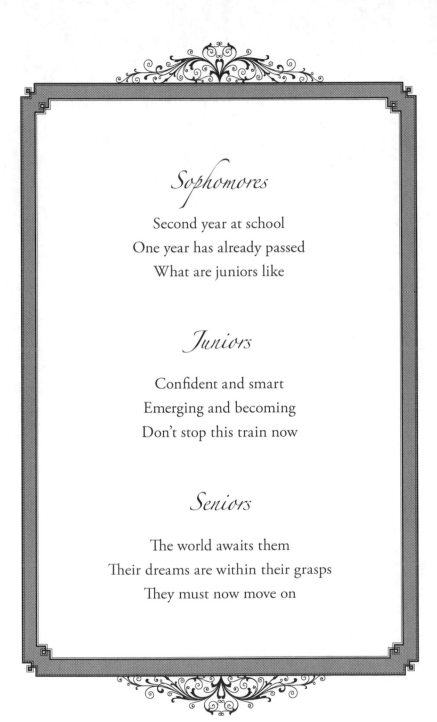

Sophomores

Second year at school
One year has already passed
What are juniors like

Juniors

Confident and smart
Emerging and becoming
Don't stop this train now

Seniors

The world awaits them
Their dreams are within their grasps
They must now move on

Adolescence

Their first try at love
Sometimes it works, sometimes not
It's fun to watch though

Gambles

We must all take them
Calculated are the best
A fool takes the rest

Youthful

Youthfulness deceives
We think it will last always
But today I'm old

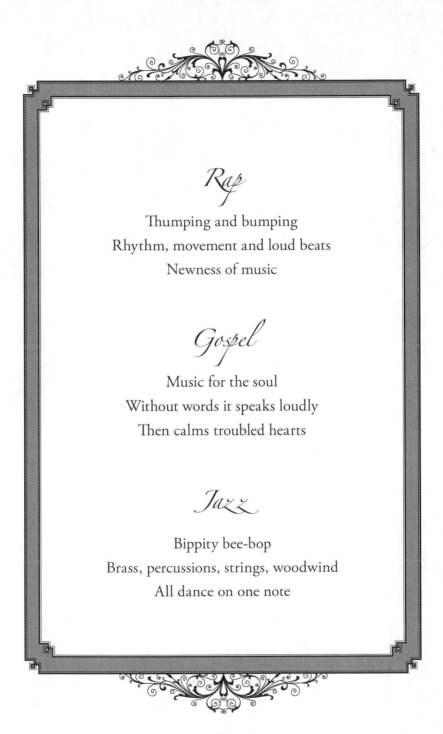

Rap

Thumping and bumping
Rhythm, movement and loud beats
Newness of music

Gospel

Music for the soul
Without words it speaks loudly
Then calms troubled hearts

Jazz

Bippity bee-bop
Brass, percussions, strings, woodwind
All dance on one note

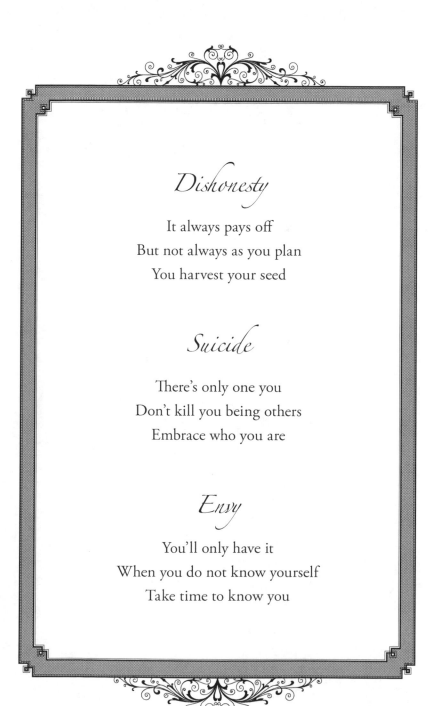

Dishonesty

It always pays off
But not always as you plan
You harvest your seed

Suicide

There's only one you
Don't kill you being others
Embrace who you are

Envy

You'll only have it
When you do not know yourself
Take time to know you

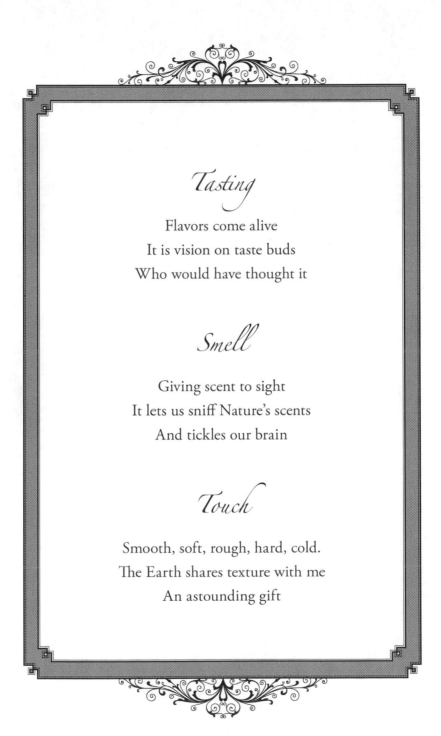

Tasting

Flavors come alive
It is vision on taste buds
Who would have thought it

Smell

Giving scent to sight
It lets us sniff Nature's scents
And tickles our brain

Touch

Smooth, soft, rough, hard, cold.
The Earth shares texture with me
An astounding gift

Smiles

They say I'm o.k.
And do battle against frowns
They are contagious

Sunrise

The eye of heaven
Finds its place high over head
Then shines on us all

Competition

Don't compare yourself
You are you and they are they
Always do your best

Striving

Never cease to strive
You are one effort away
Don't you dare give up

Champions

Adorned with medals
Smiles replacing painful tears
A long time coming

Parents

They are our teachers
Children must know they're not friends
Parents do your job

Generations

The reason for genes
Traits of many are in you
You're a composite

Blessings

Created for you
Someone loves you just that much
Be thankful for them

Abuse

Why do we do it
It comes from not knowing Truth
You're your own victim

Race

Black, white, brown, yellow
Peel away the coverings
And what do you have

Mythology

What's real and what's not
Nothing is quite as it seems
Can you tell what's real

Ambitions

They are what drive us
Without them people stagnant
They power our will

Home

It's not just a house
It's more than just pretty things
It's where I am loved

Babies

Innocence in flesh
We owe them the very best
Love them with your all

Tolerance

It's not accepting
It's permitting to exist
Though the heart's unchanged

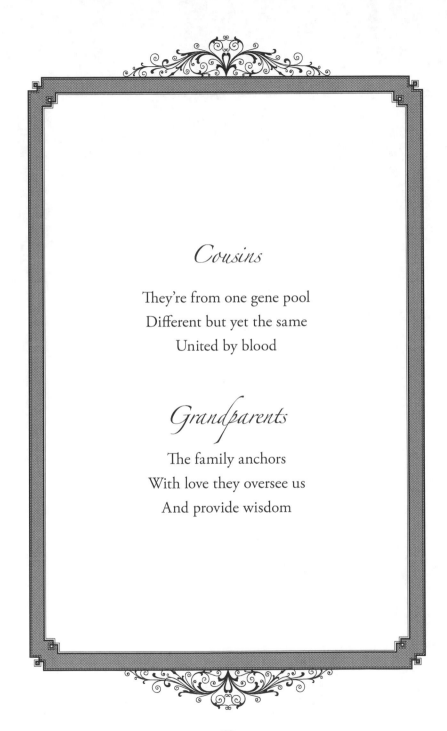

Cousins

They're from one gene pool
Different but yet the same
United by blood

Grandparents

The family anchors
With love they oversee us
And provide wisdom

Notes

Believing the ears to be a major portal to our basis of understanding and belief, Samuel Williams has compiled a number of original didactic haiku poems for his readers to read, enjoy and pass on. The power of his words coupled with the grace of his delivery and the artistry of his unique teaching skills all combine to enlighten, inspire, and instruct in the form of these simple seventeen syllable haiku poems. His wisdom and obvious love for and intent on sharing his insight into a variety of issues are clearly obvious and masterfully conveyed.

Home

It's not just a house
It's more than just pretty things
It's where I am loved

Smiles

They say I'm okay
And do battle against frowns
They are contagious

Youthful

Youthfulness deceives
We think it will last always
But today I'm old

Author, Samuel Williams, a native of small town Wadley, Georgia (population approximately 1300), grew up wanting to become just two things in life—a journalist and a pilot. Fate obliged his desires and the now multiple times published, former helicopter pilot often glances back over his life and "thanks God" for the plight and path that brought him to this point.

Williams is a teacher in every respect of the word. He has taught at the middle school, high school and college levels and has been honored as Star Teacher and Teacher of the Year at both the middle and high school levels. Williams, who presently teaches and resides in Yokosuka, Japan, continues to inspire young people and adults alike through his didactic writings and weekly inspirational teachings.

He is the author of several works to include four books of original plays, a book of inspirational writings, a book of contemporary poetry, a novel and other works. A noted inspirational and motivational speaker, Williams is often a featured speaker at a variety of events, to include religious services and special occasions and events, and can be contacted at his email address, manifestnow1@yahoo.com or by writing to PSC 473 Box 3014, FPO, AP 96349 or 118 Maple Creek Dr., Martinez, GA 30907.